Sweet Serenity
Hello Gorgeous

Jennene Christine Obremski

Copyright © 2012 Author Name

All rights reserved.

ISBN: **10:1973873206**

ISBN-**13:978-1973873204**

DEDICATION

This book is dedicated to my support group Always A Voice and especially my pwipwis wate ajengs (adored big sisters) Kathy Jones, Debra Flowers, Jill Short and Debi Greene for supporting and encouraging my art and expression.

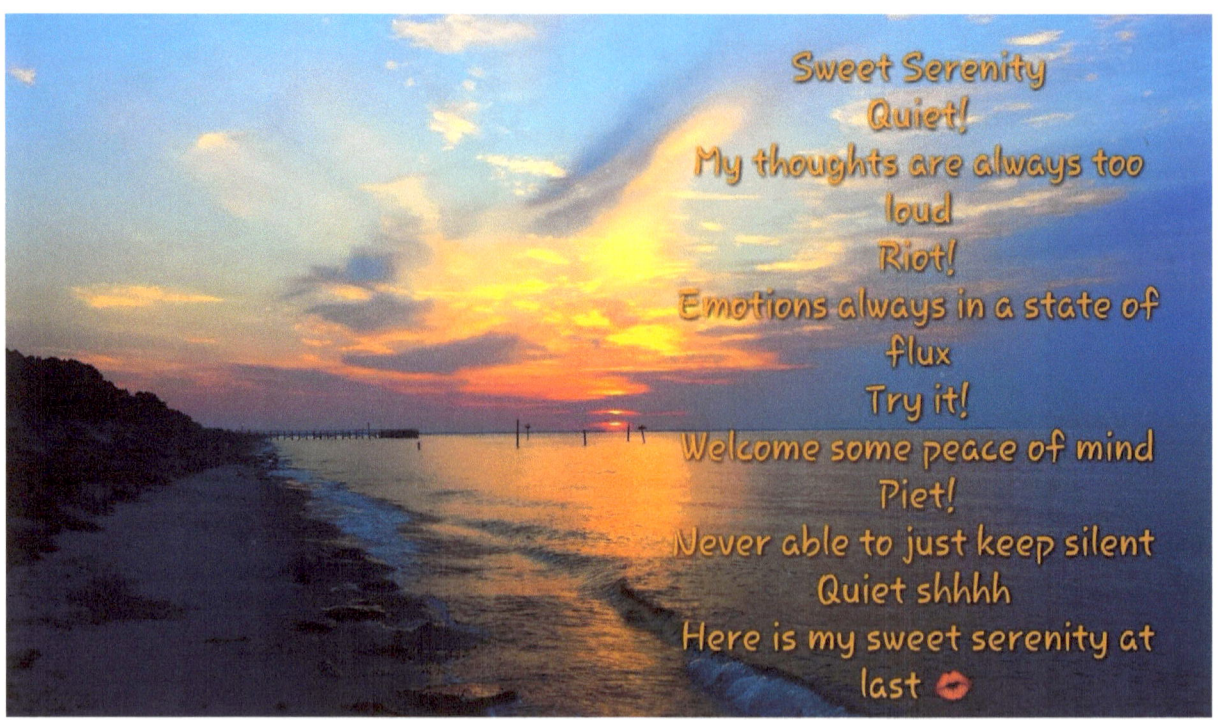

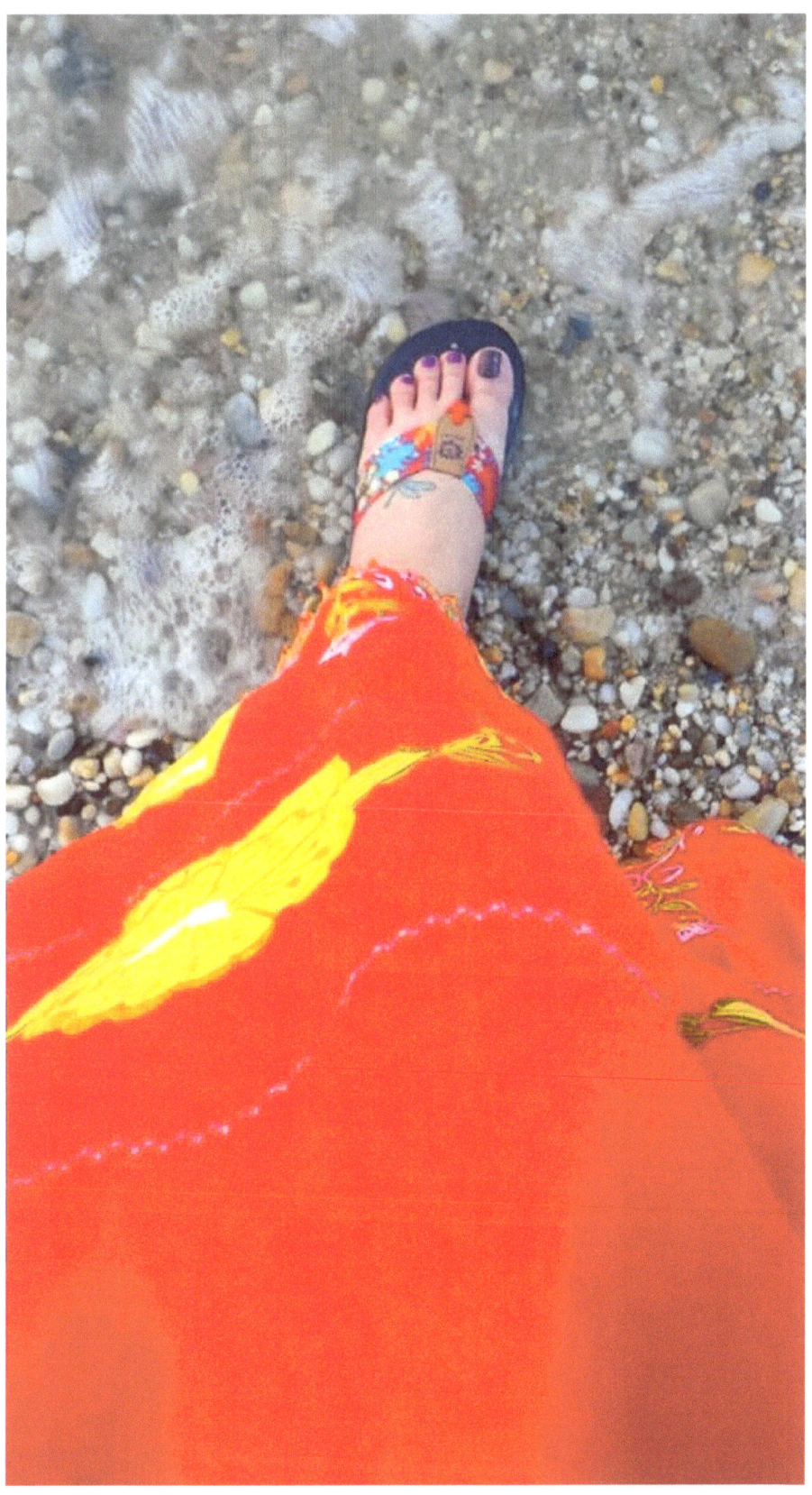

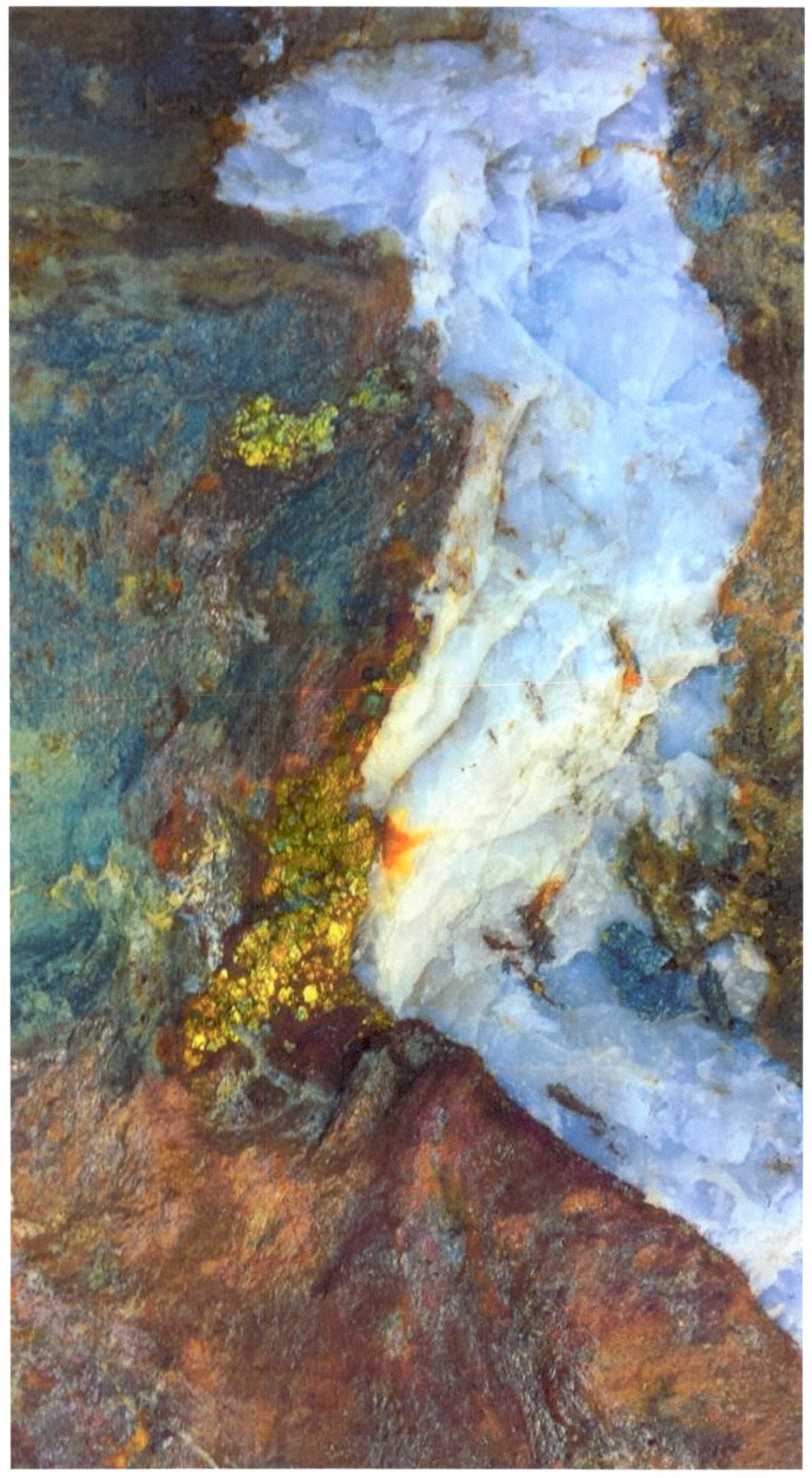

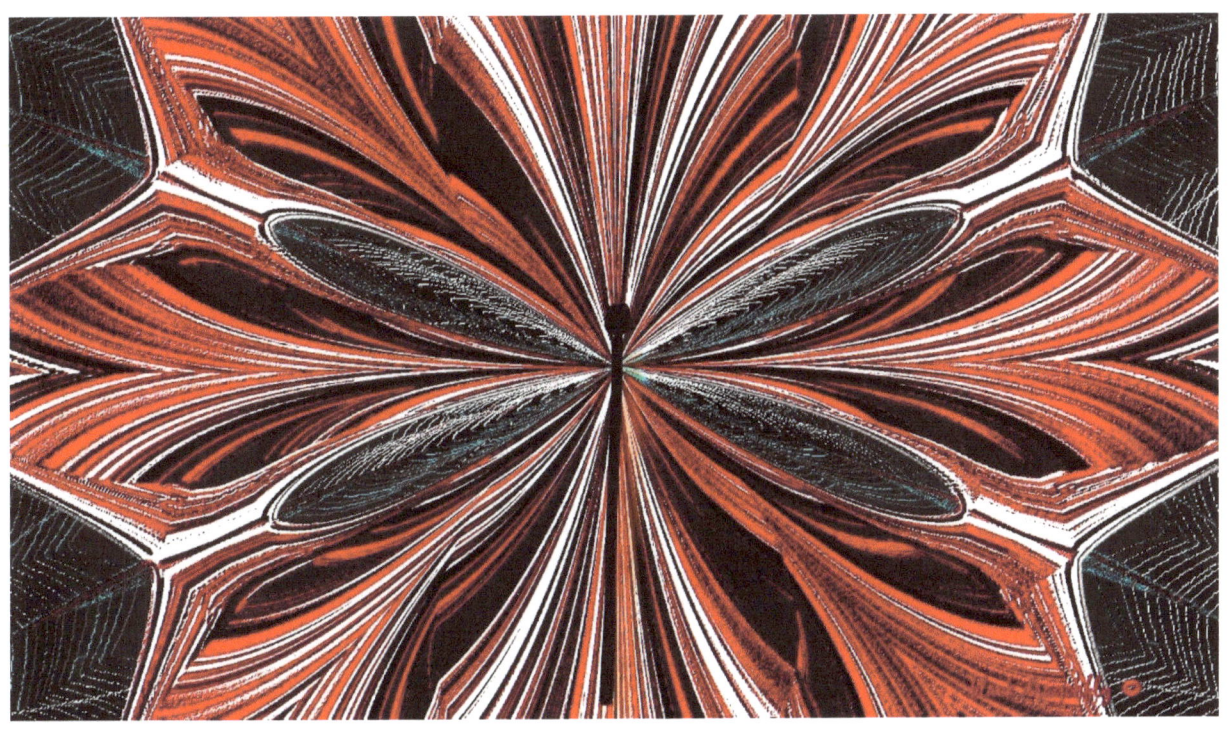

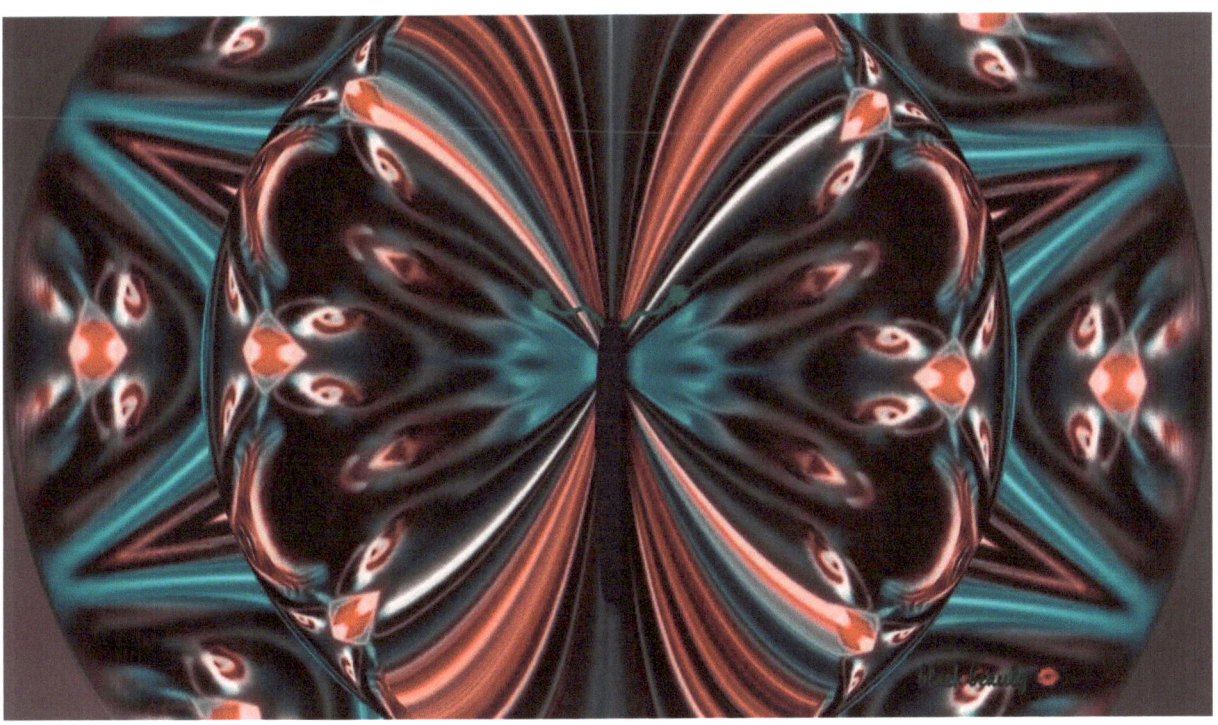

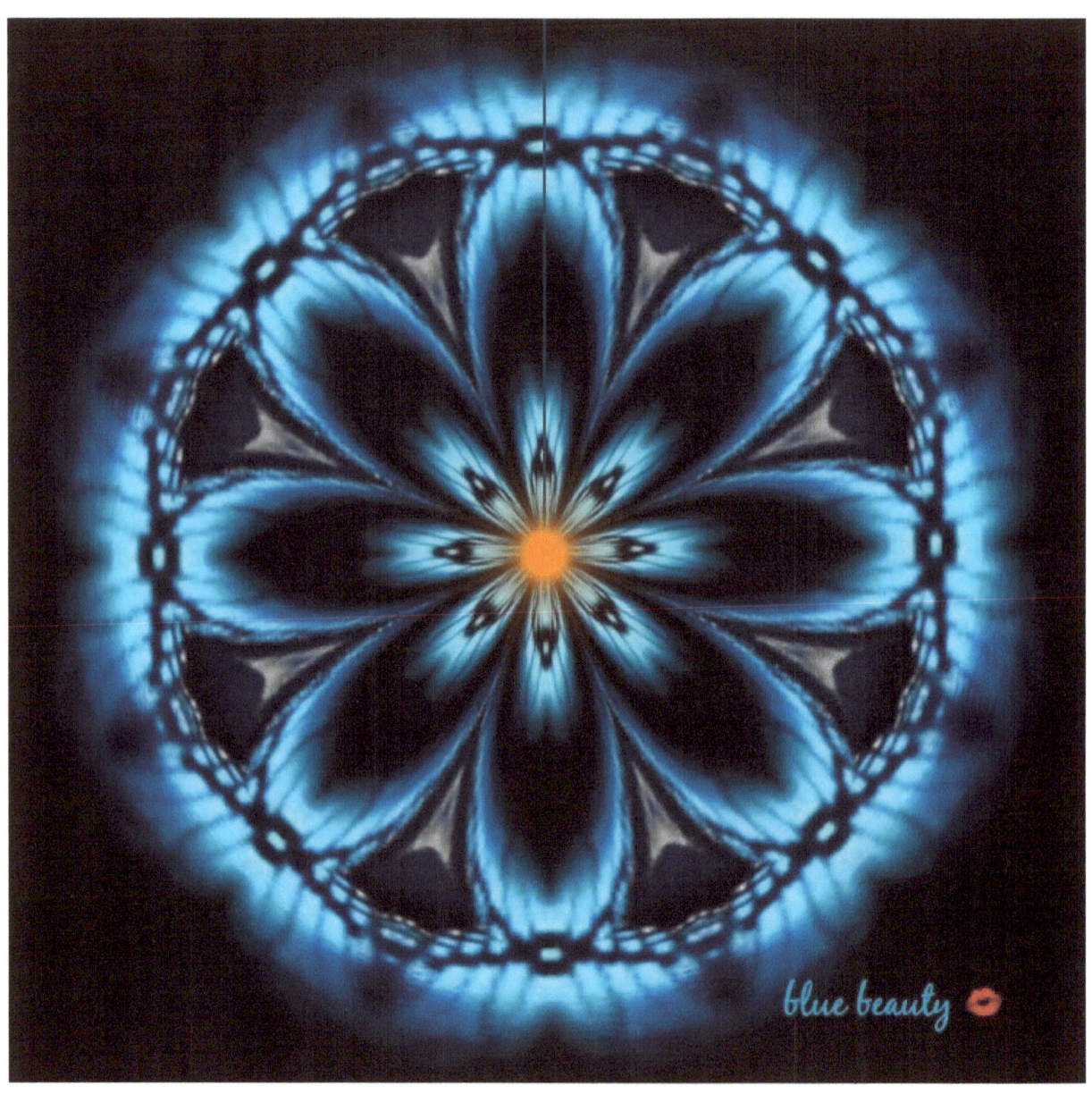

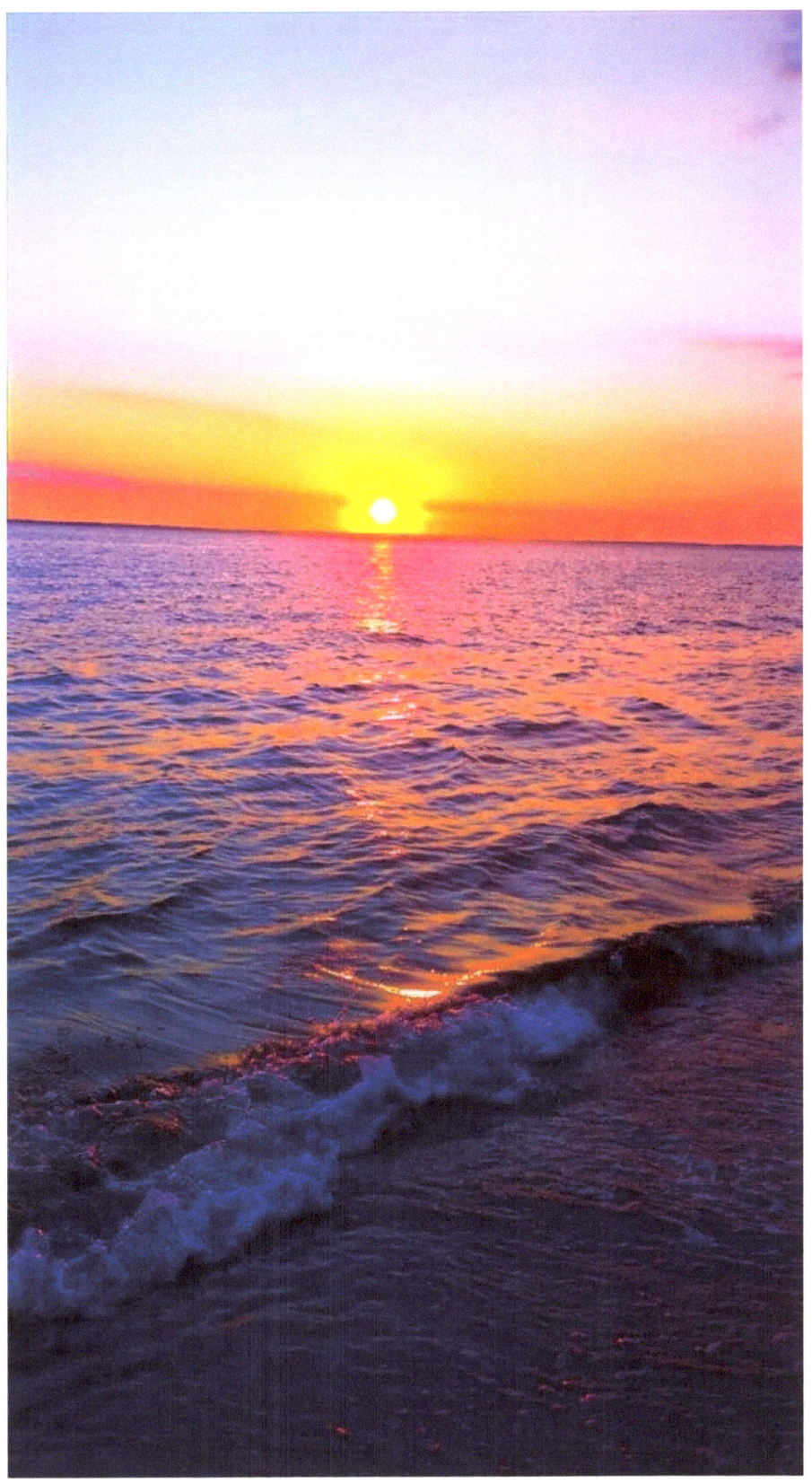

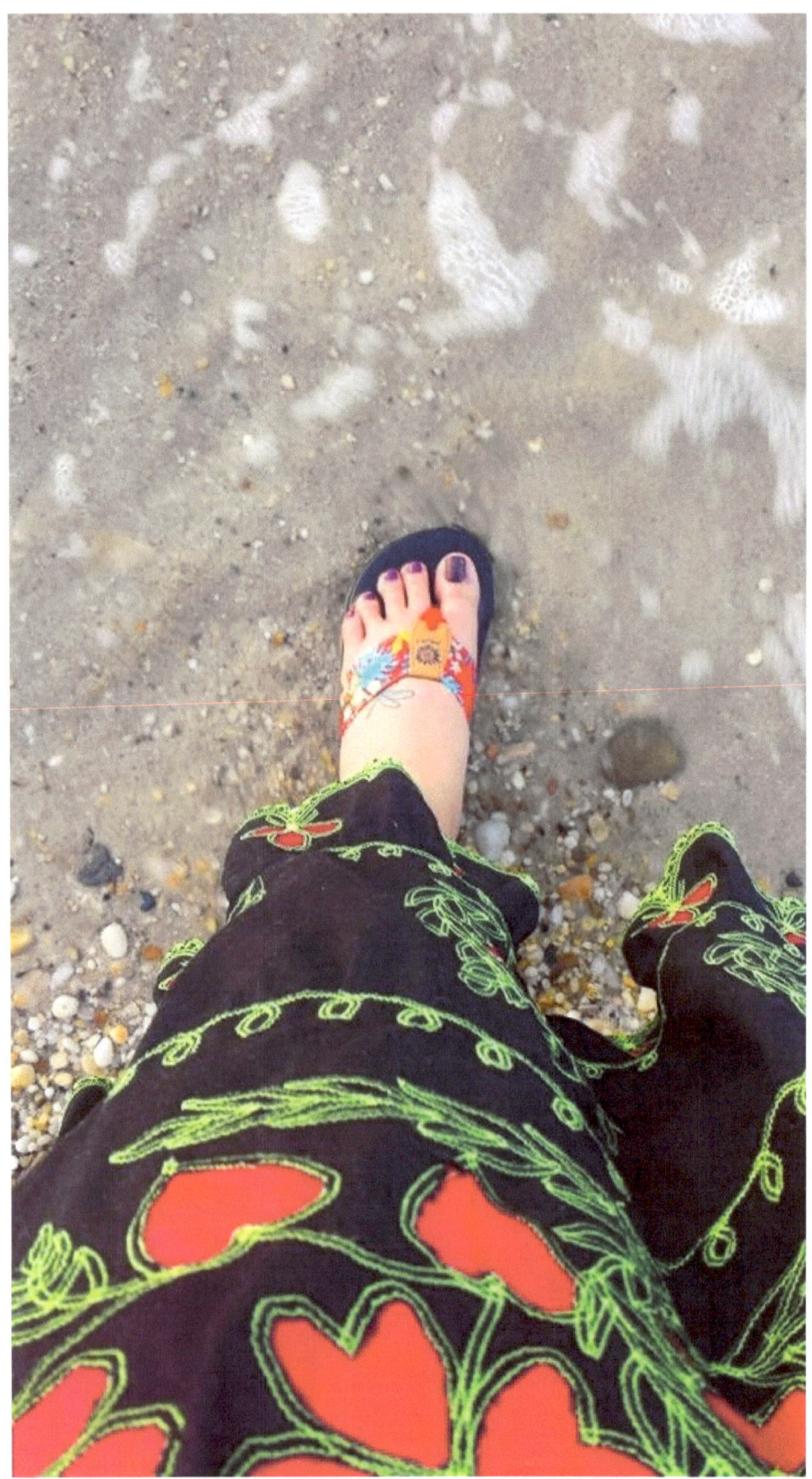

Sweet Serenity: Hello Gorgeous

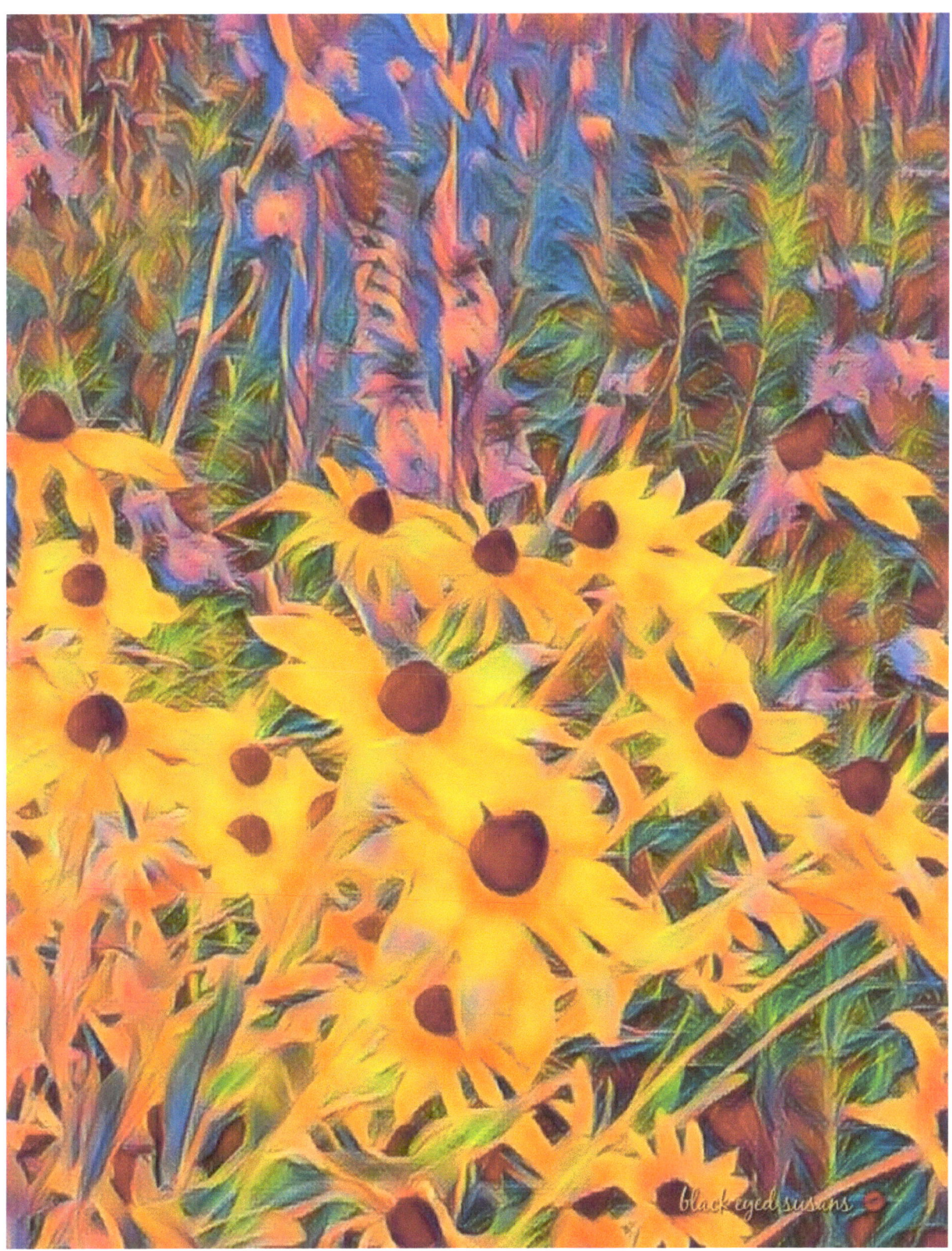

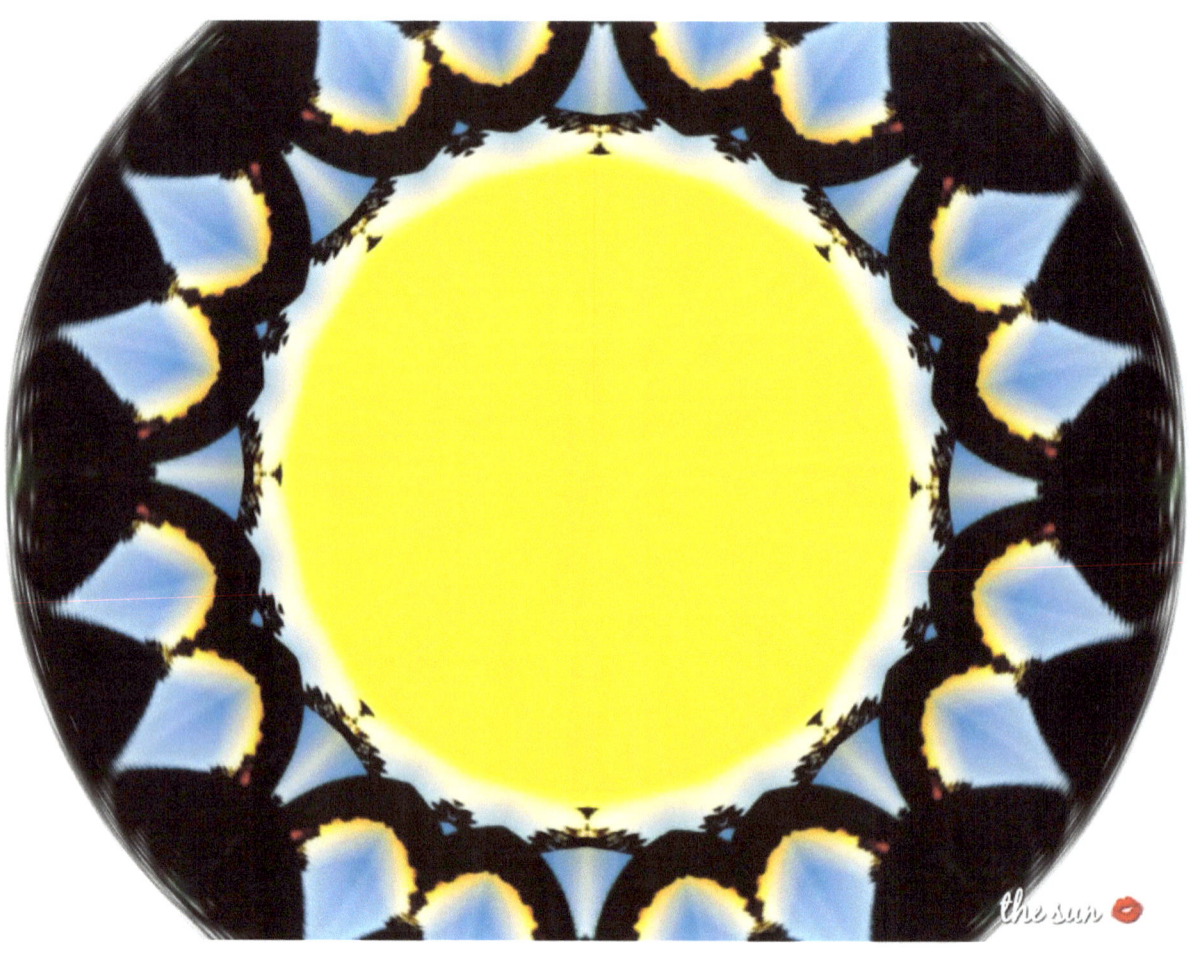

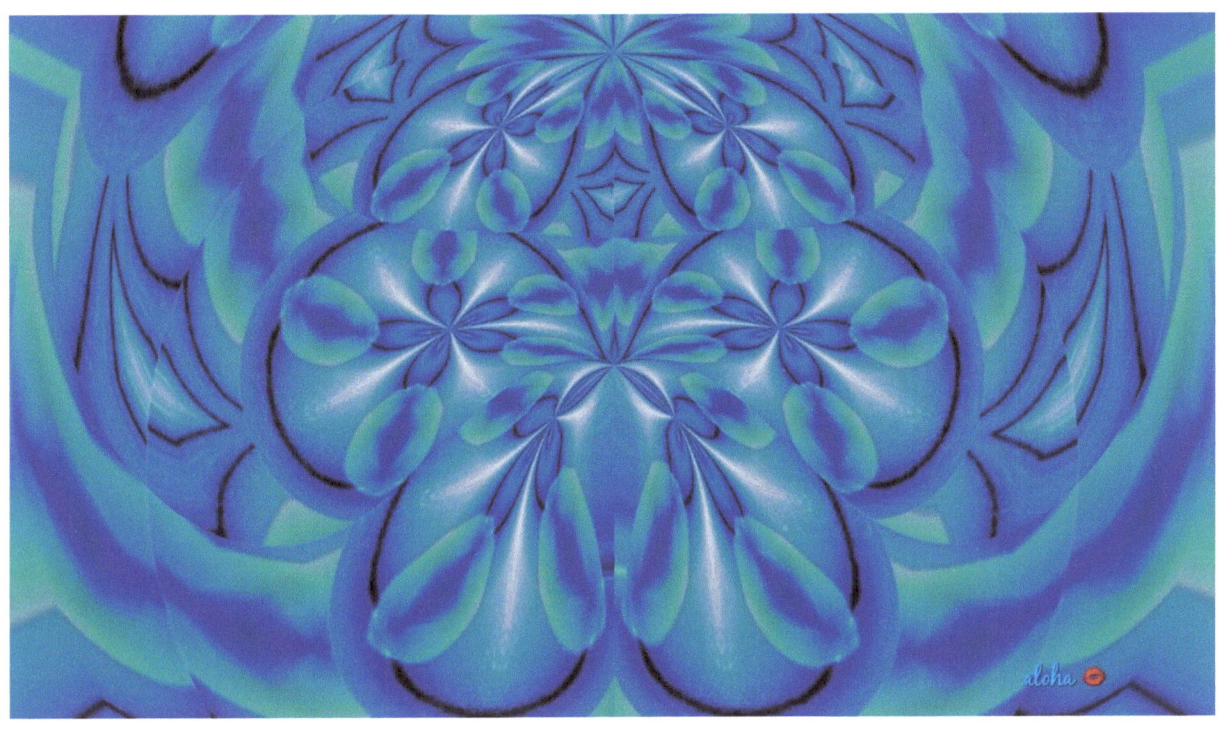
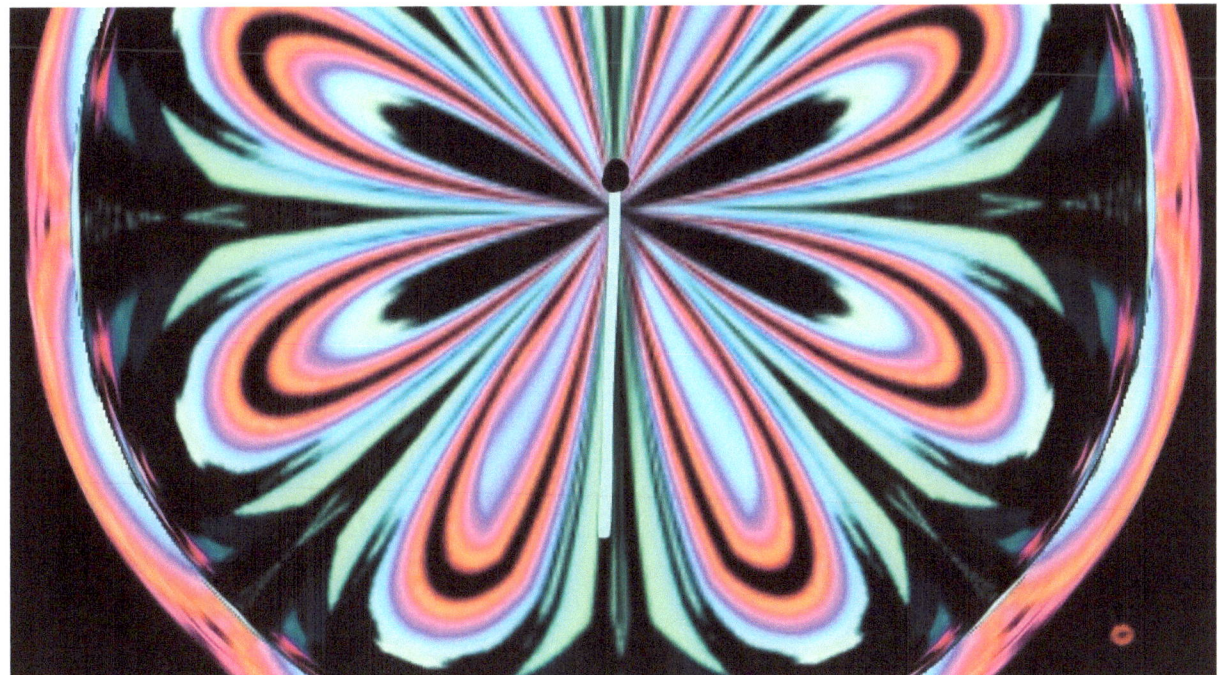

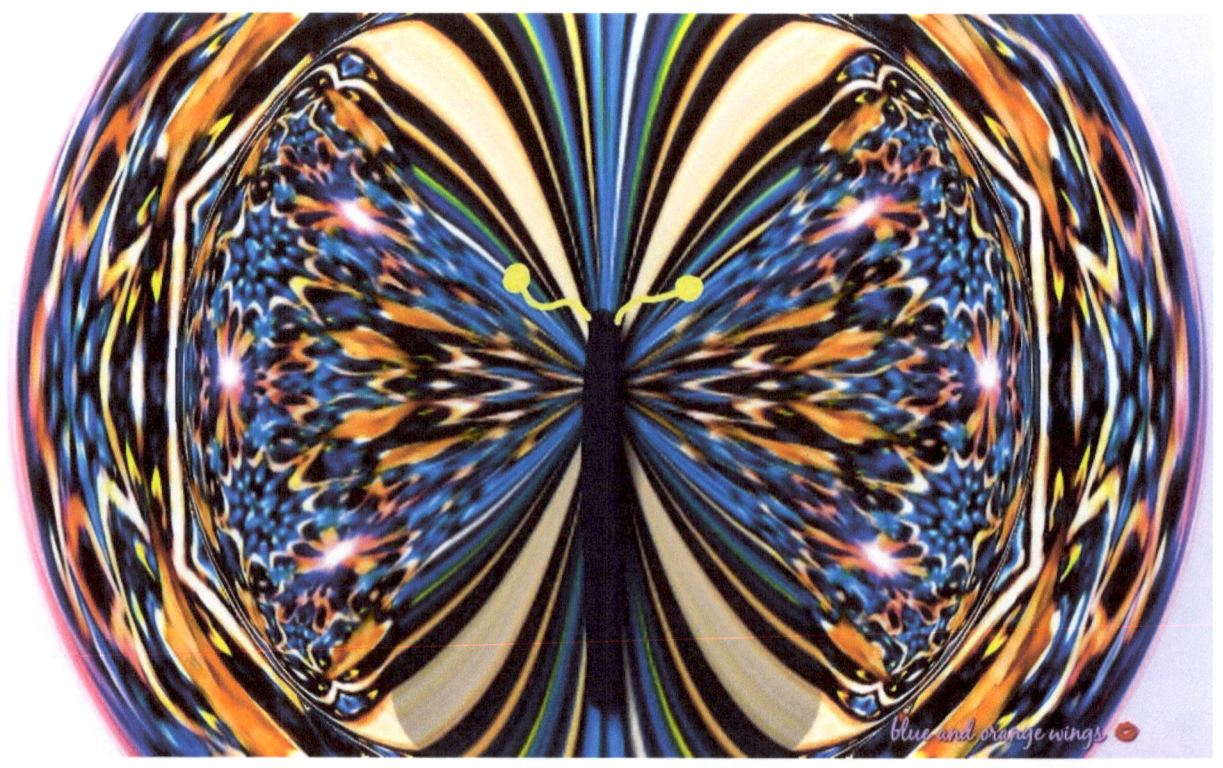

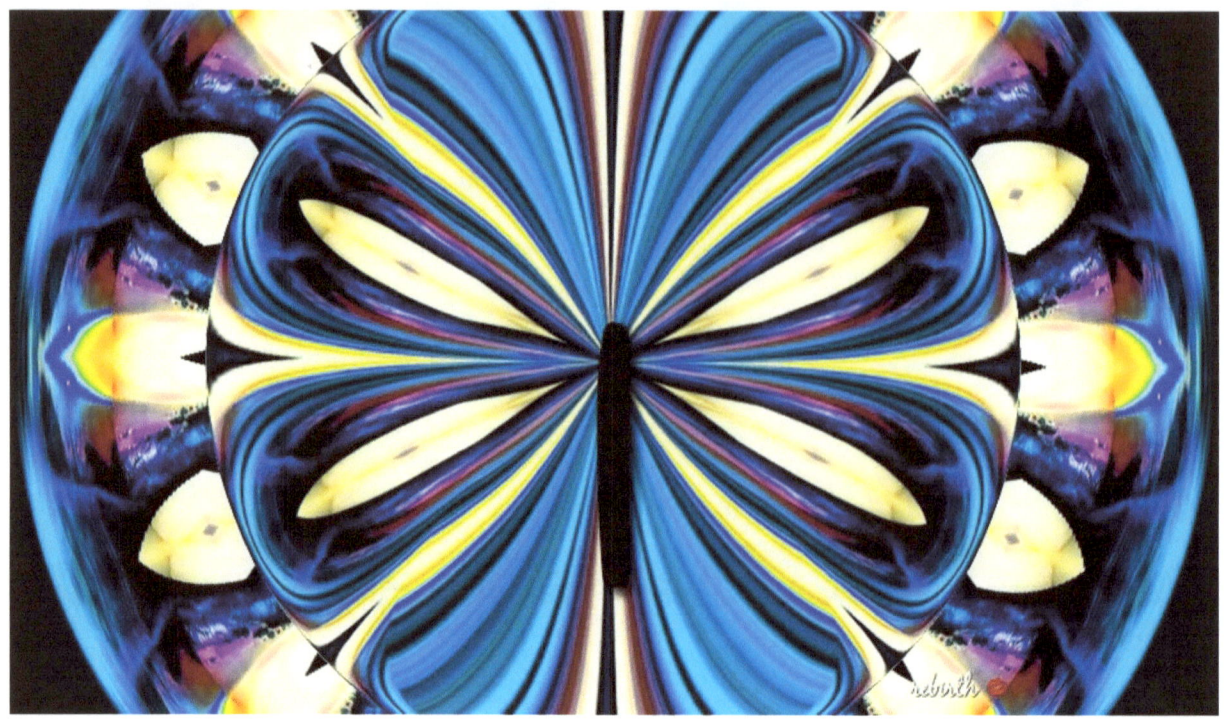

Sweet Serenity: Hello Gorgeous

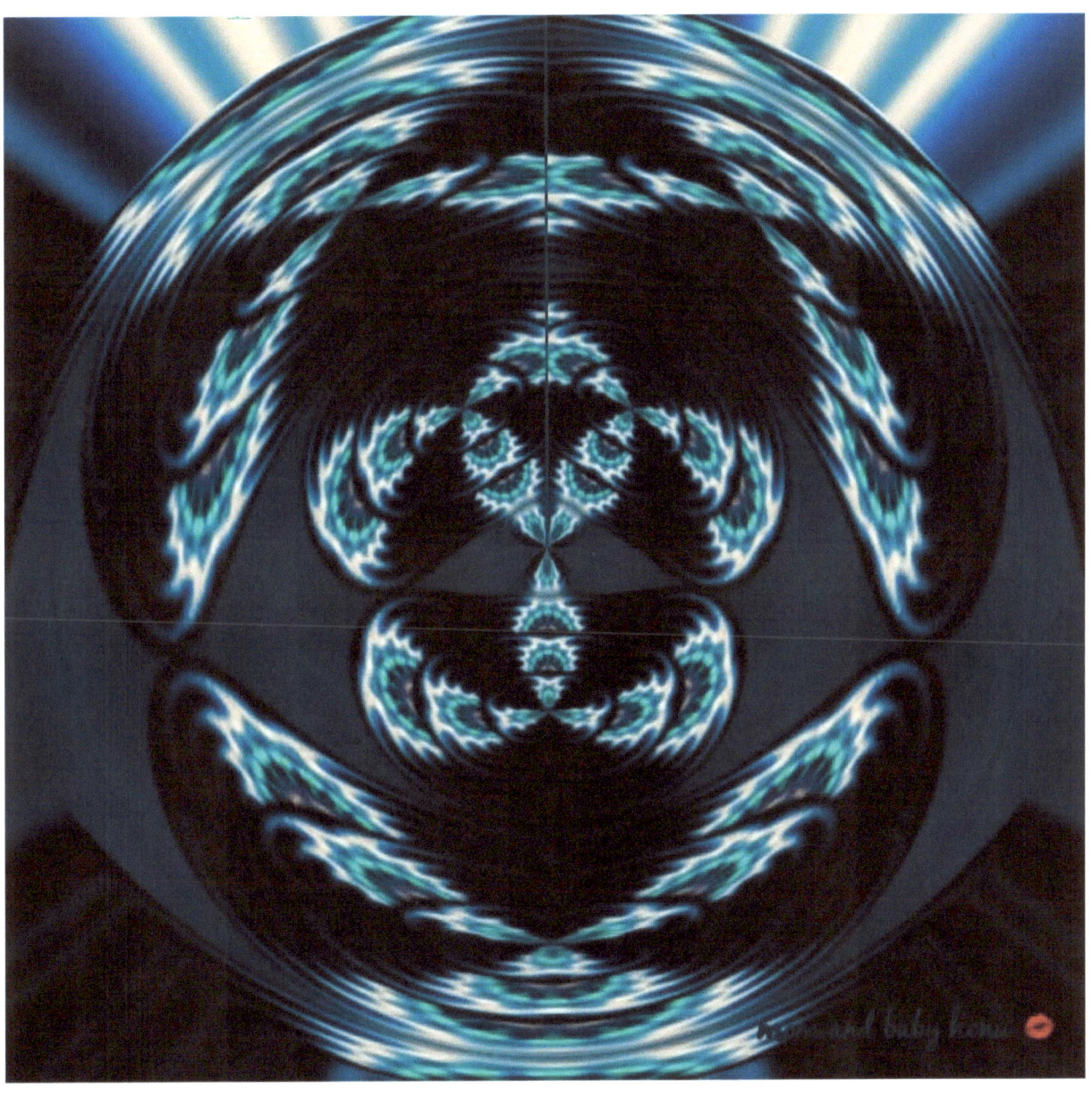

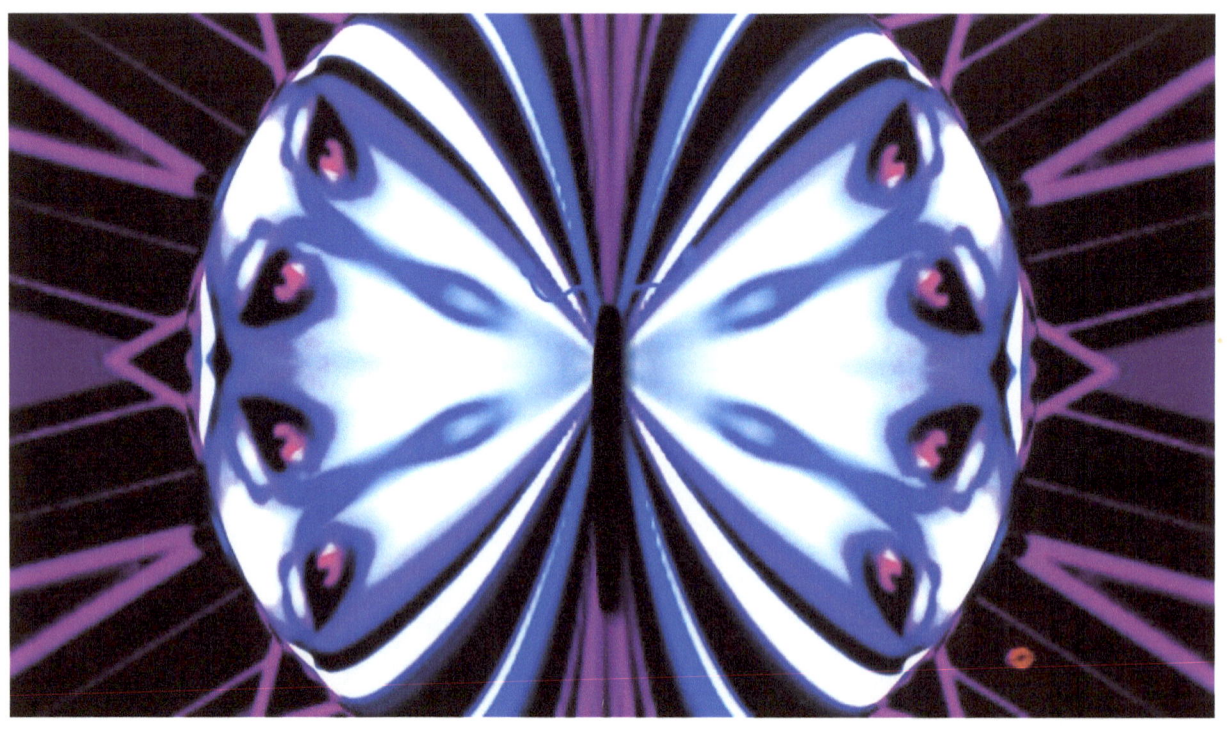

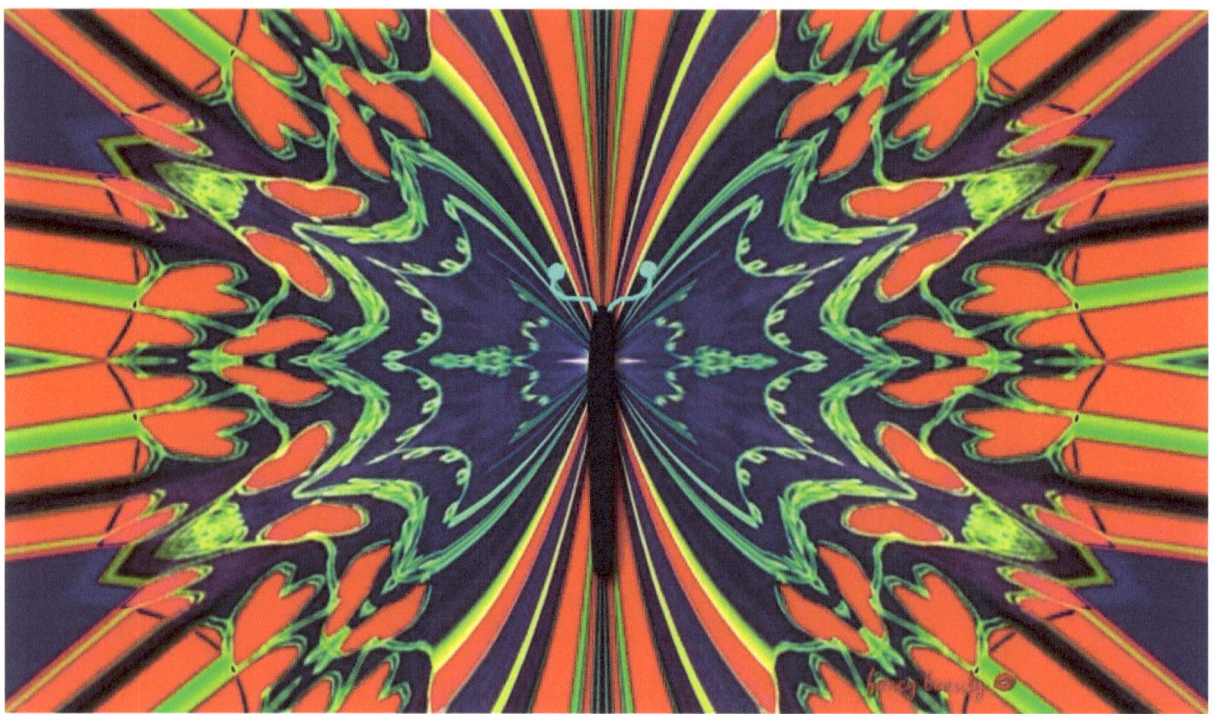

Sweet Serenity: Hello Gorgeous

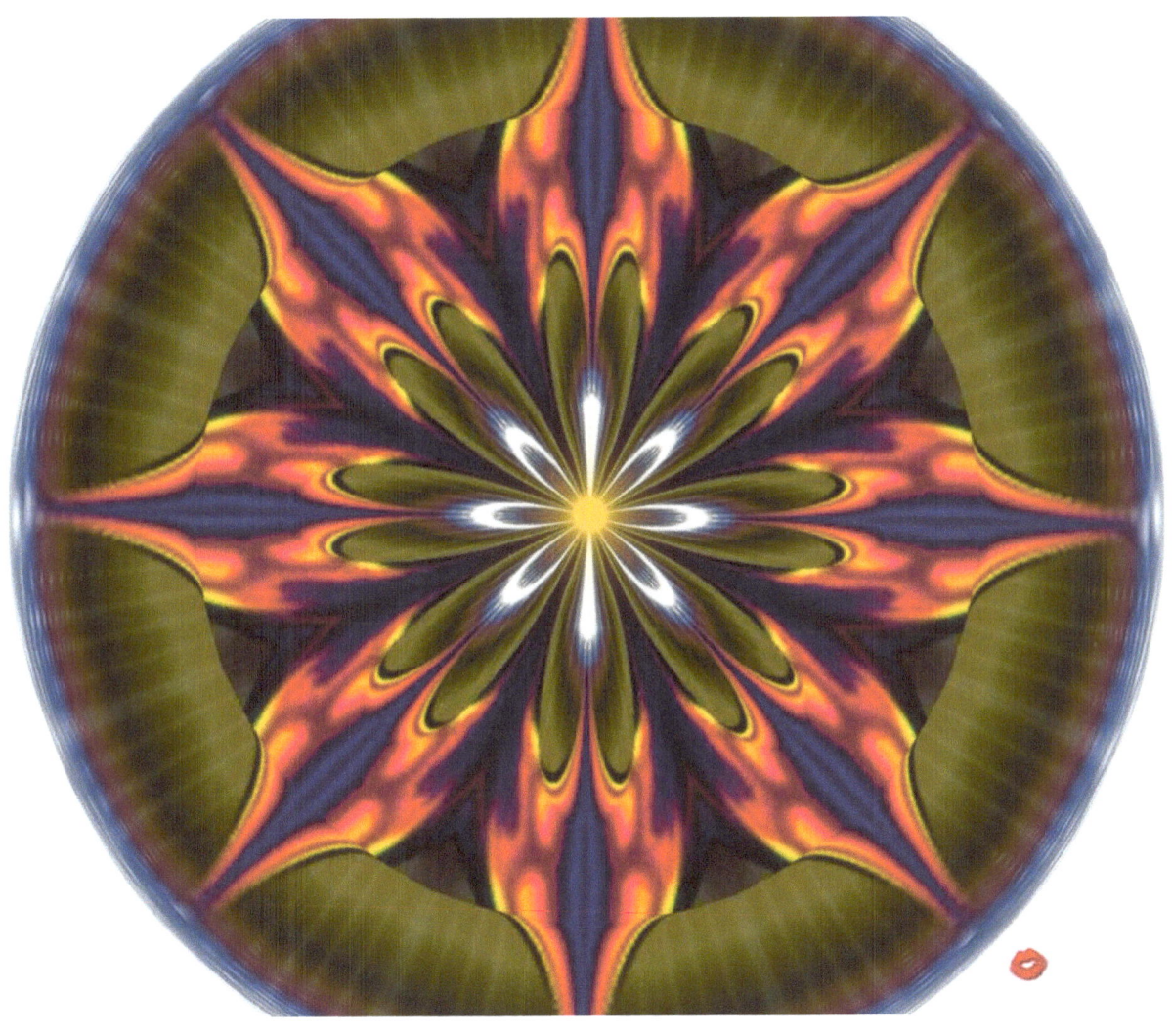

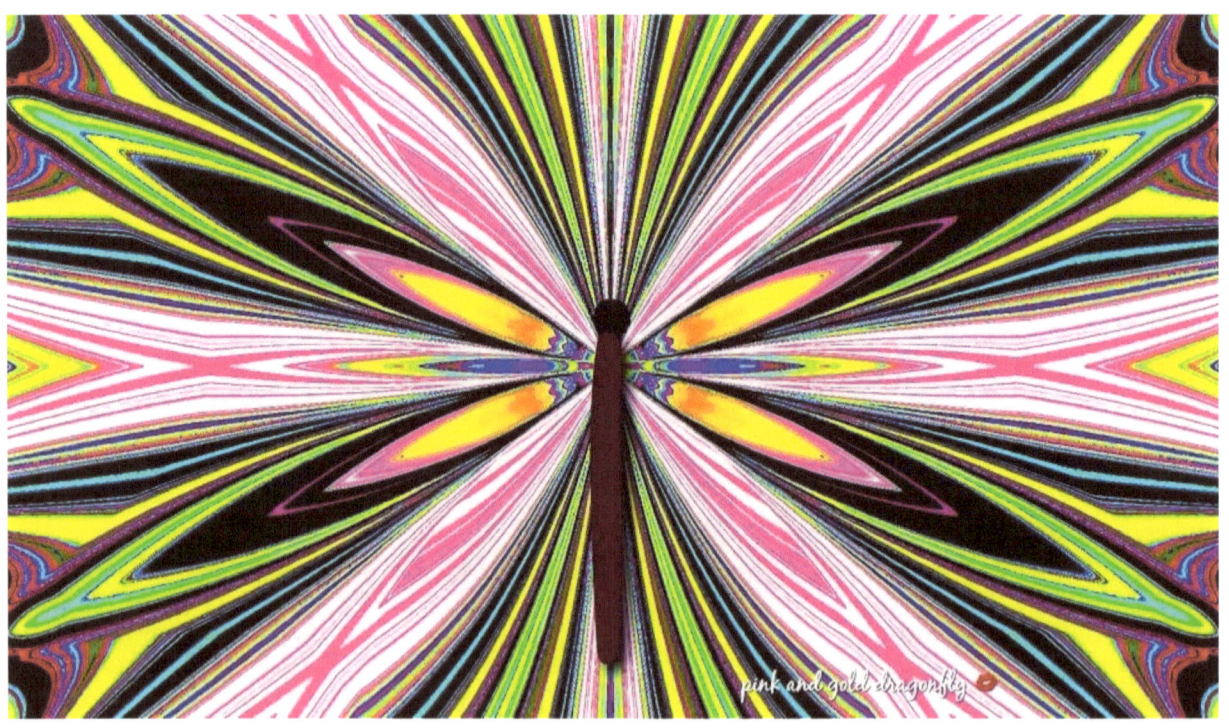

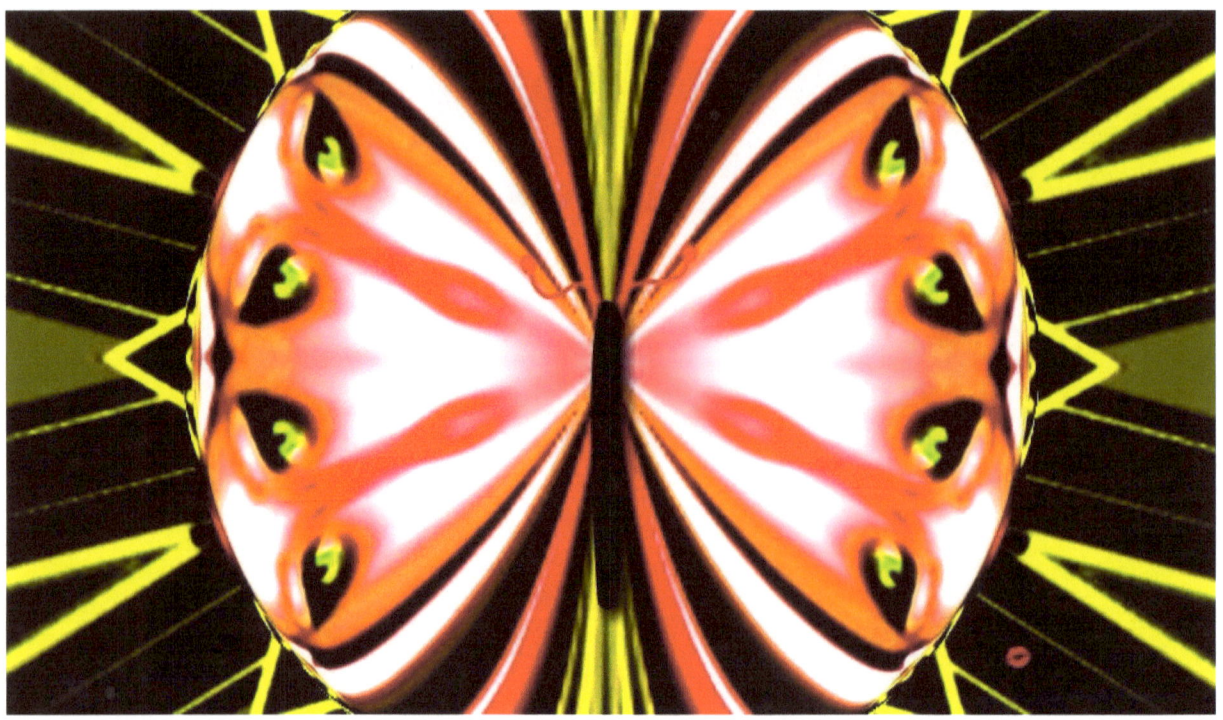

Sweet Serenity: Hello Gorgeous

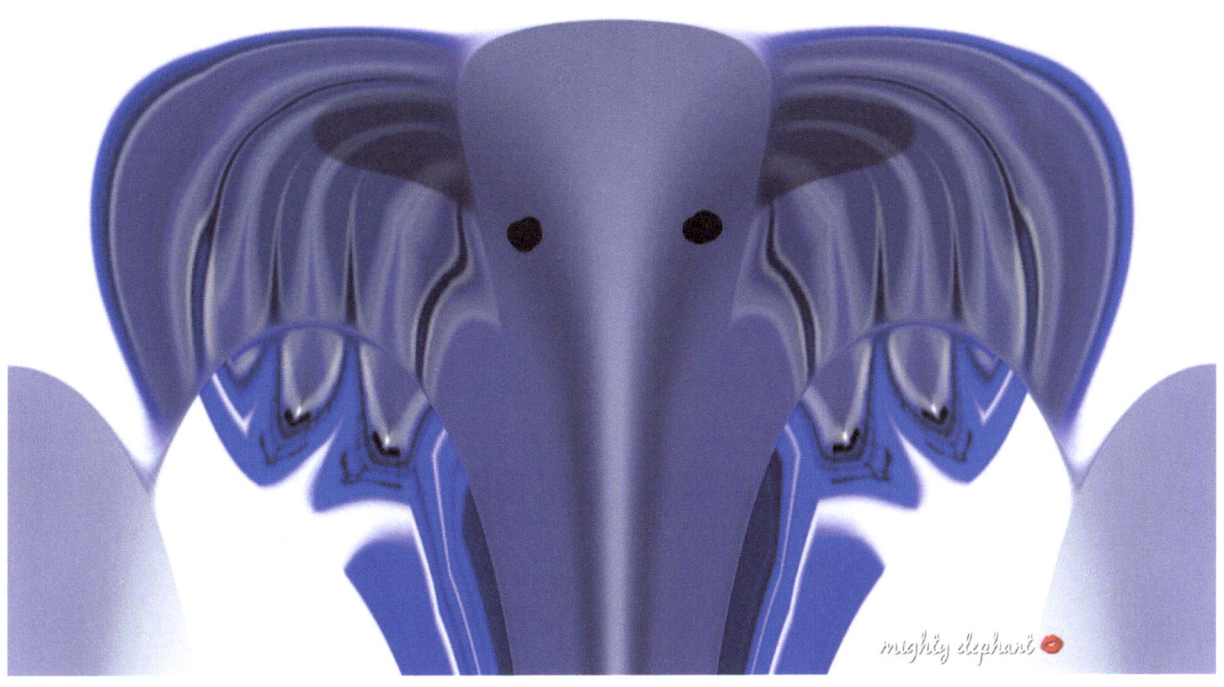

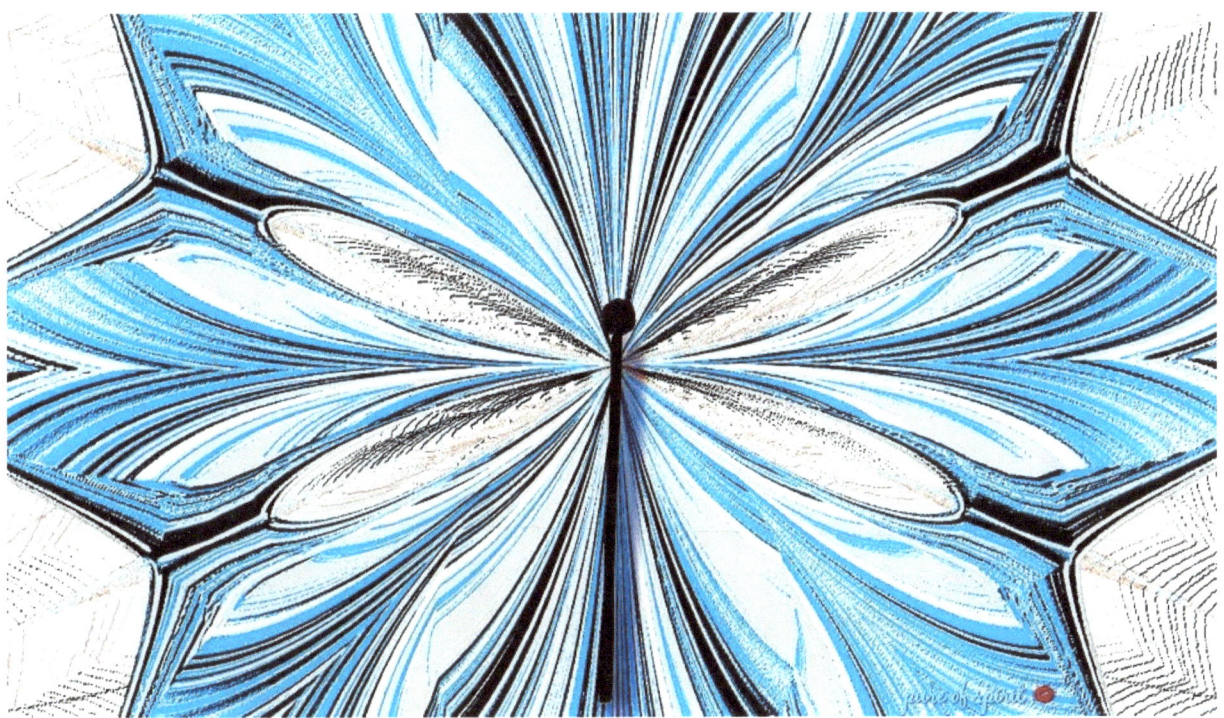

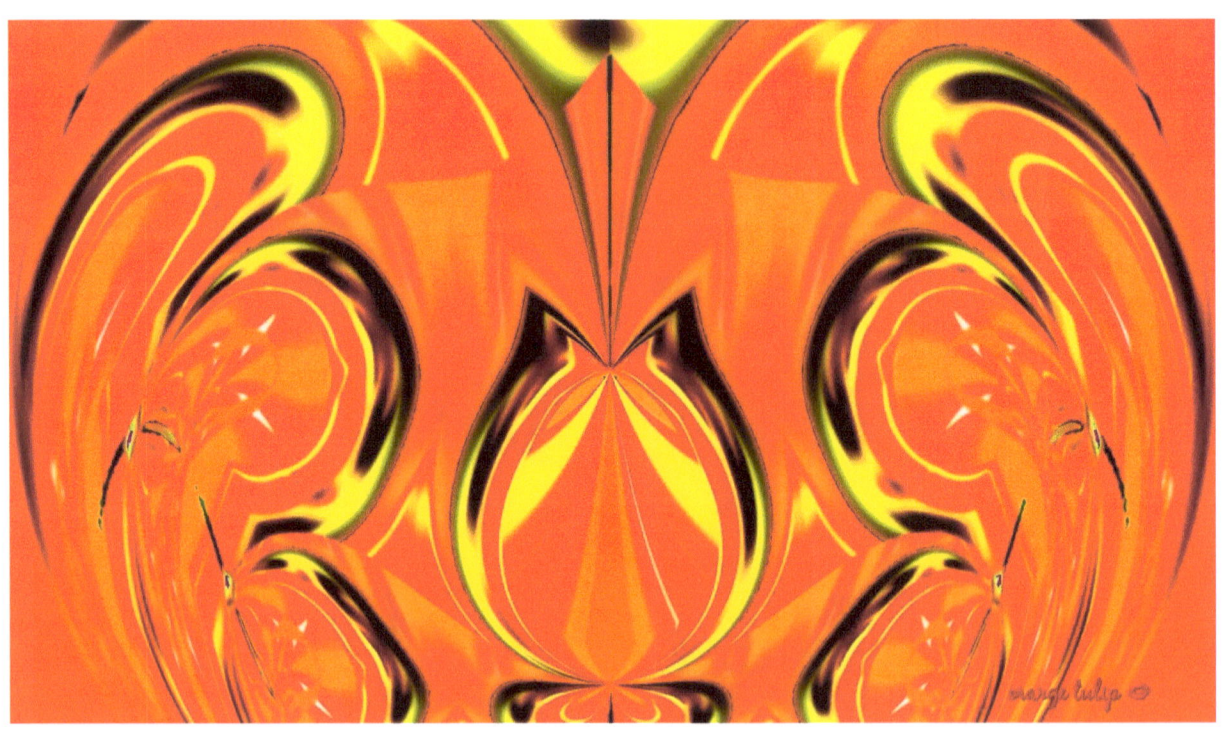

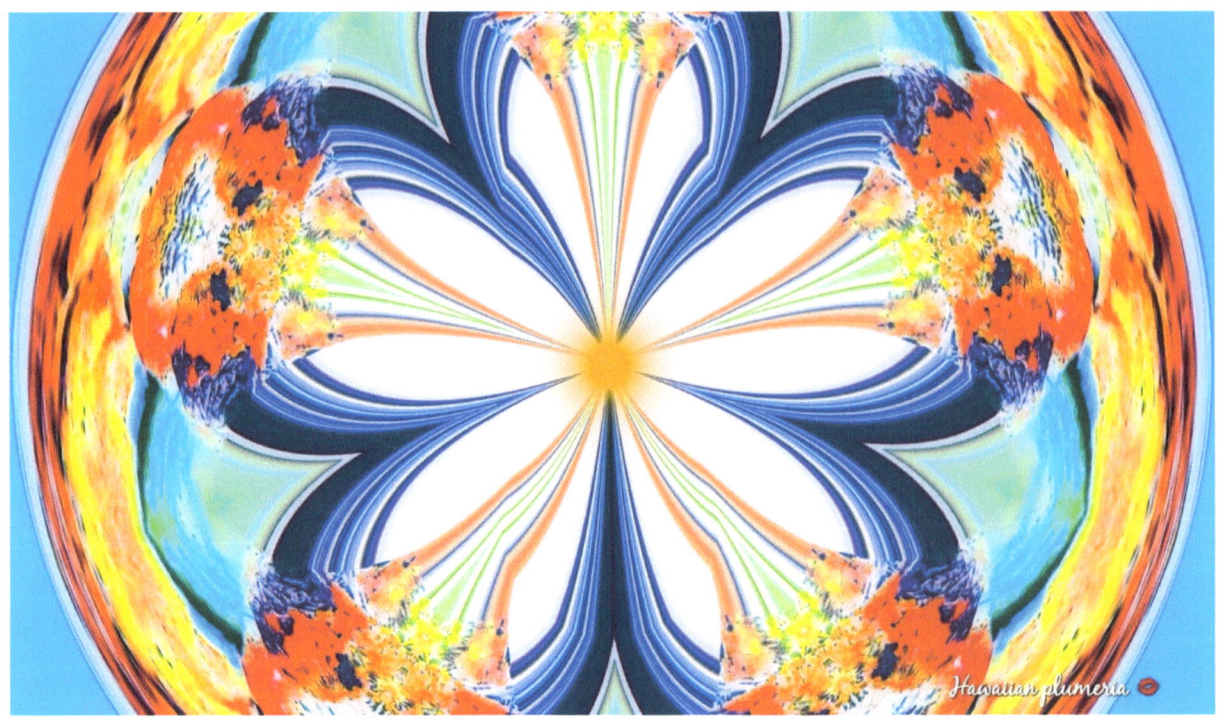

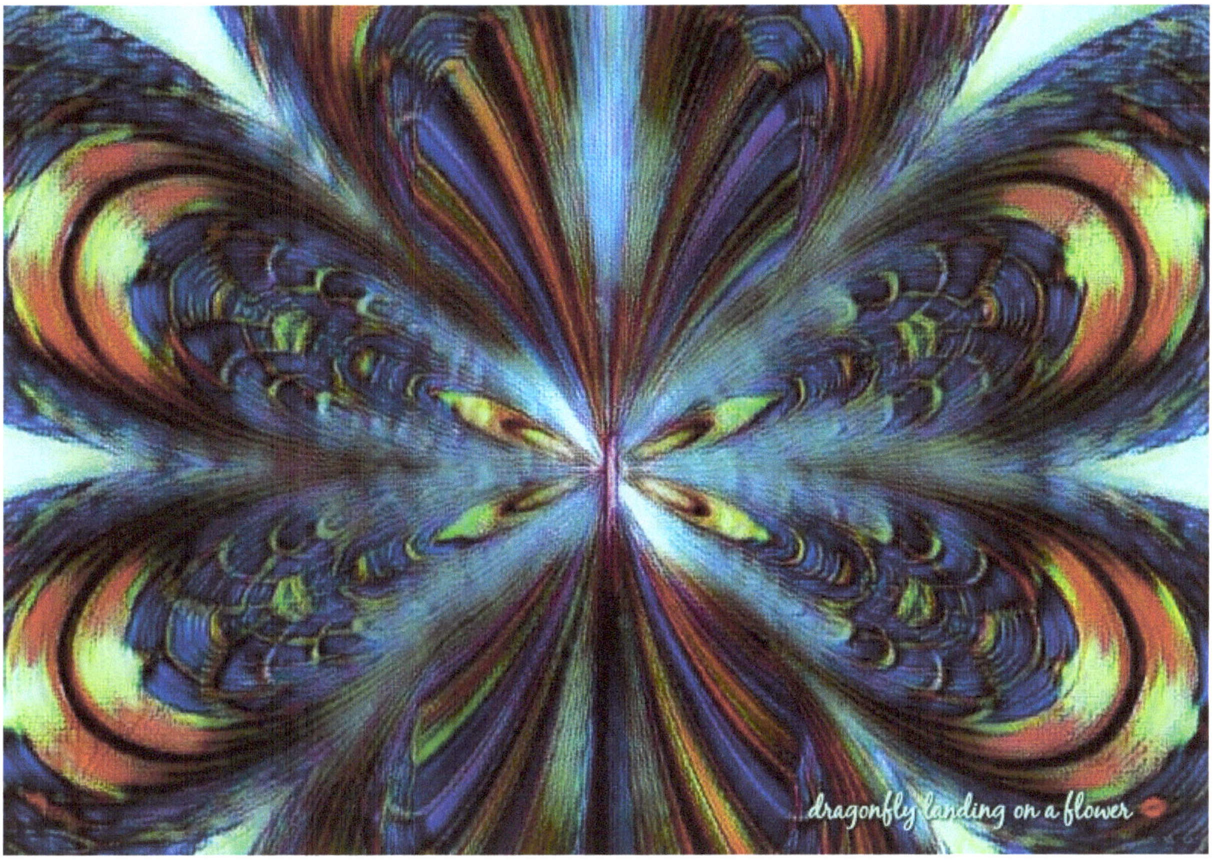

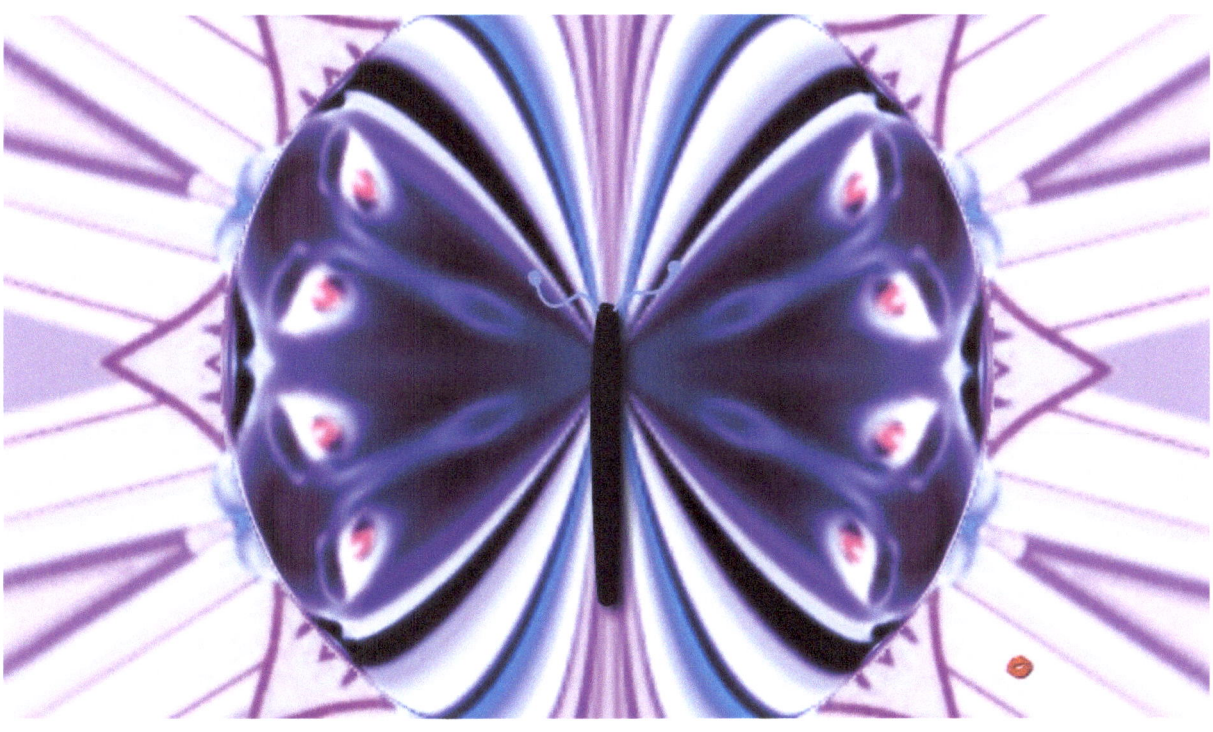

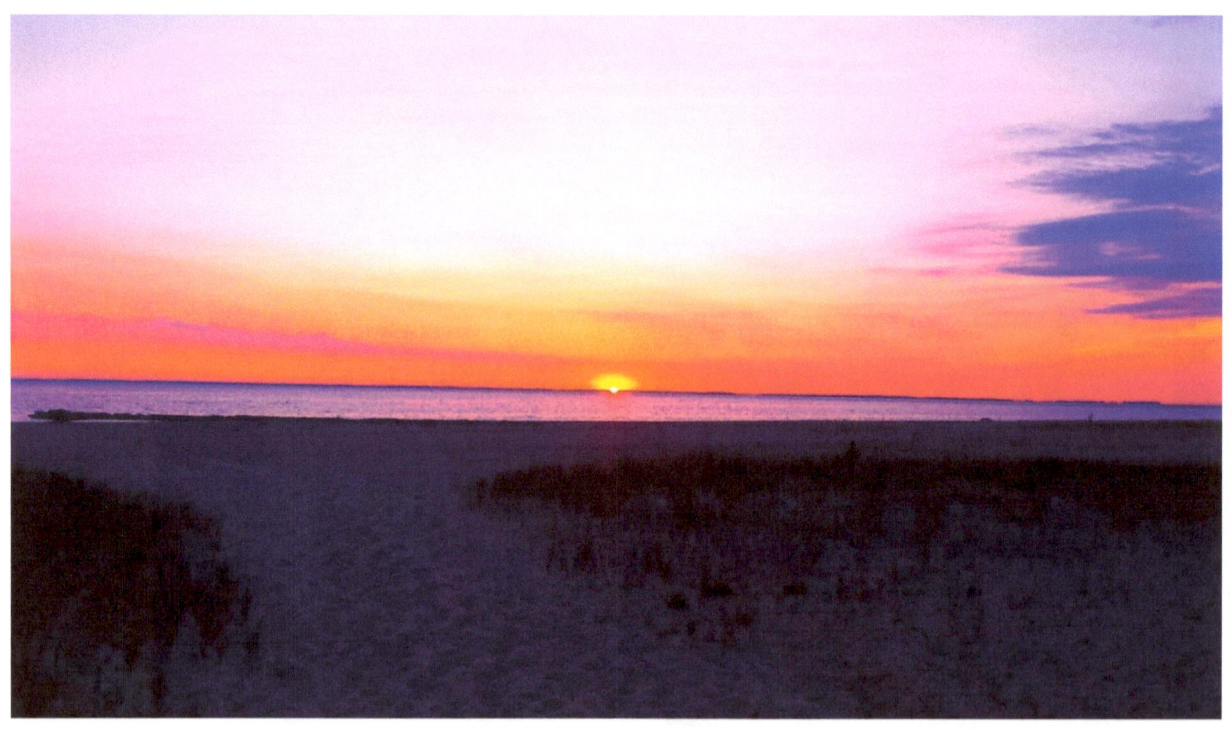
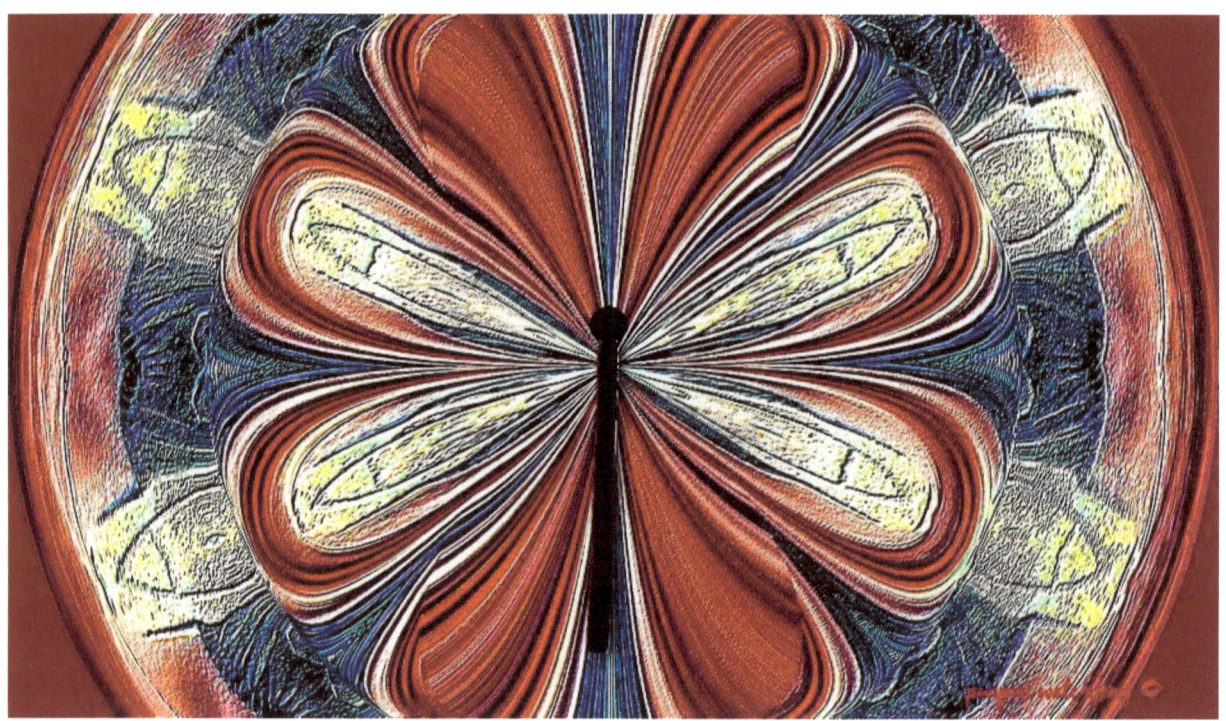

Sweet Serenity: Hello Gorgeous

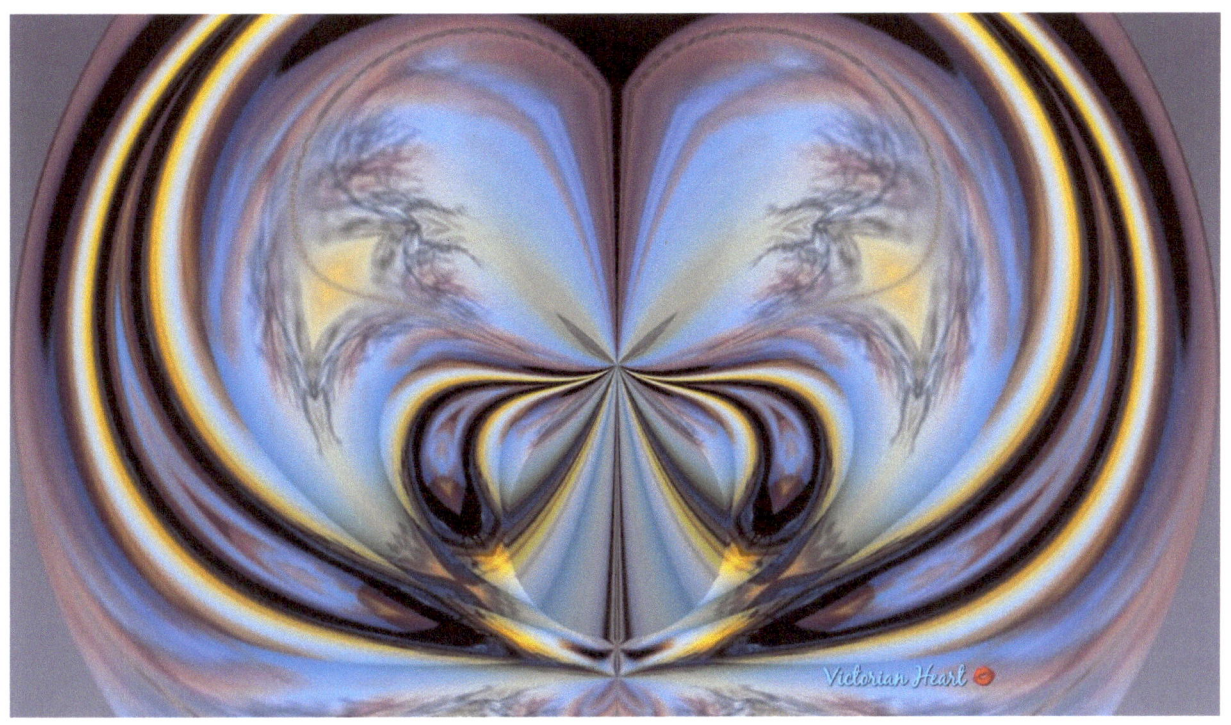

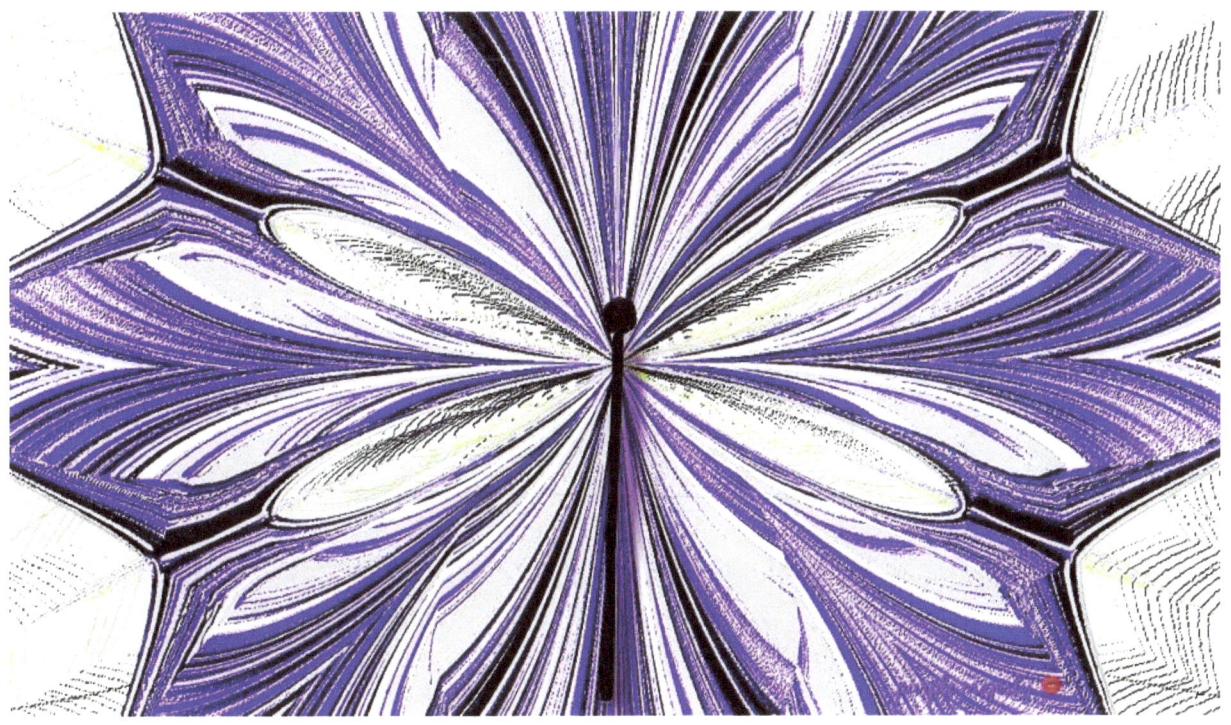

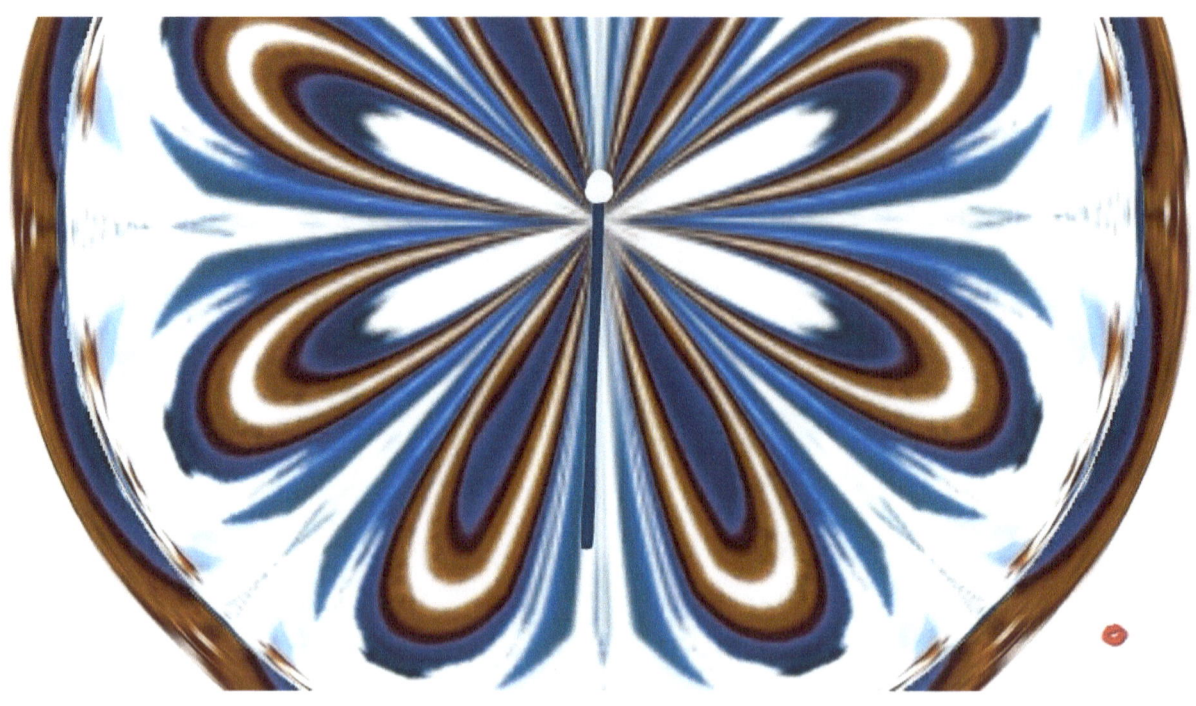
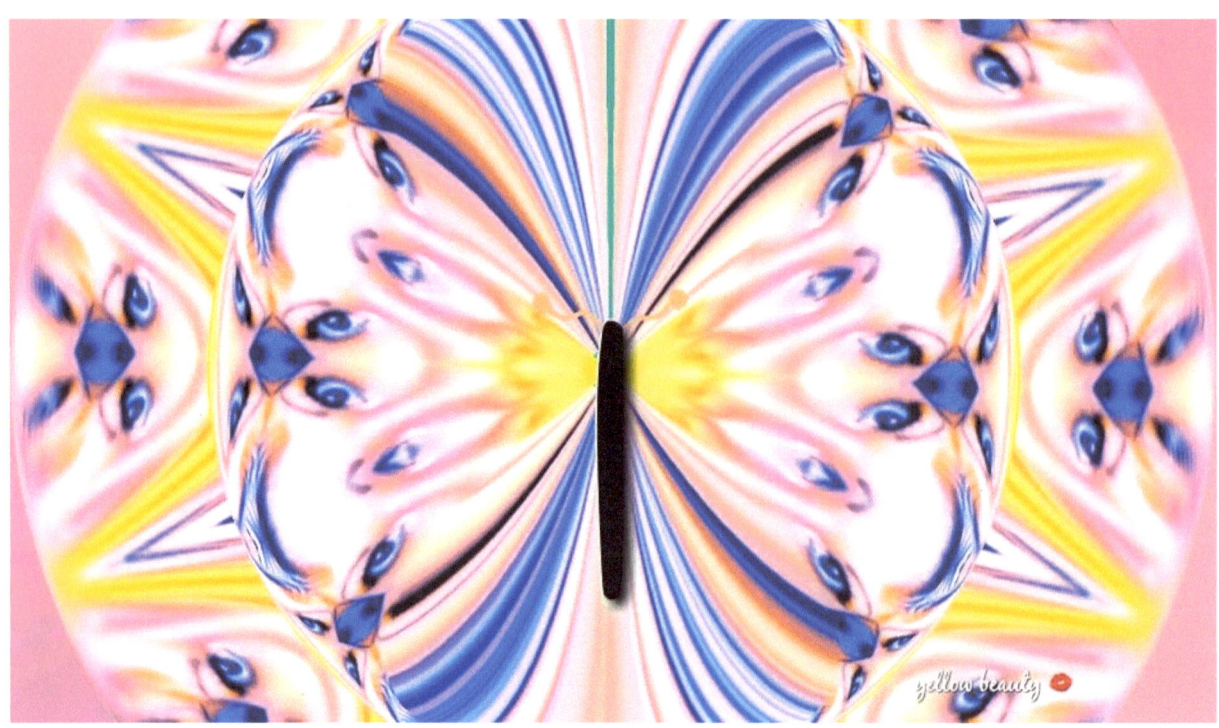

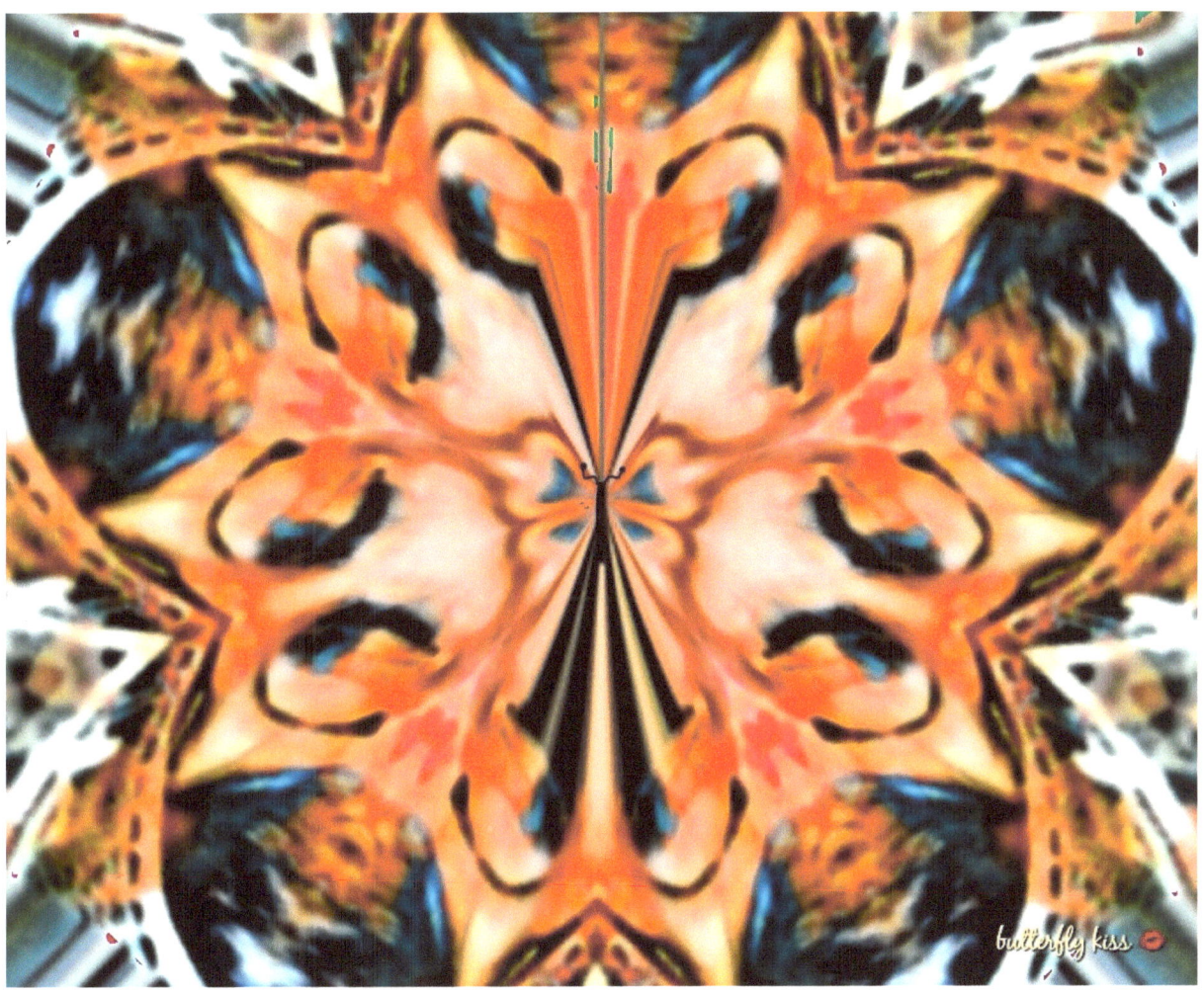

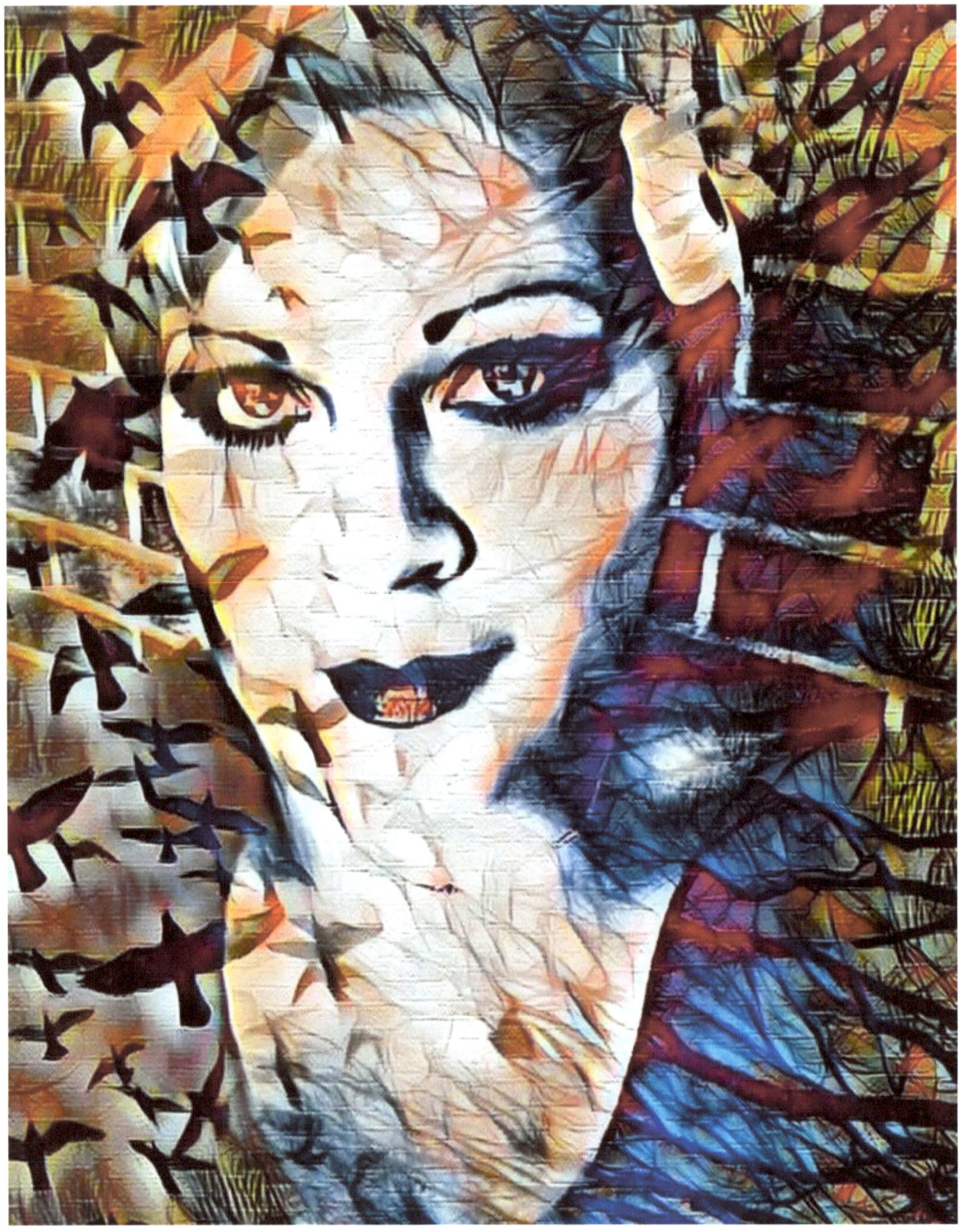

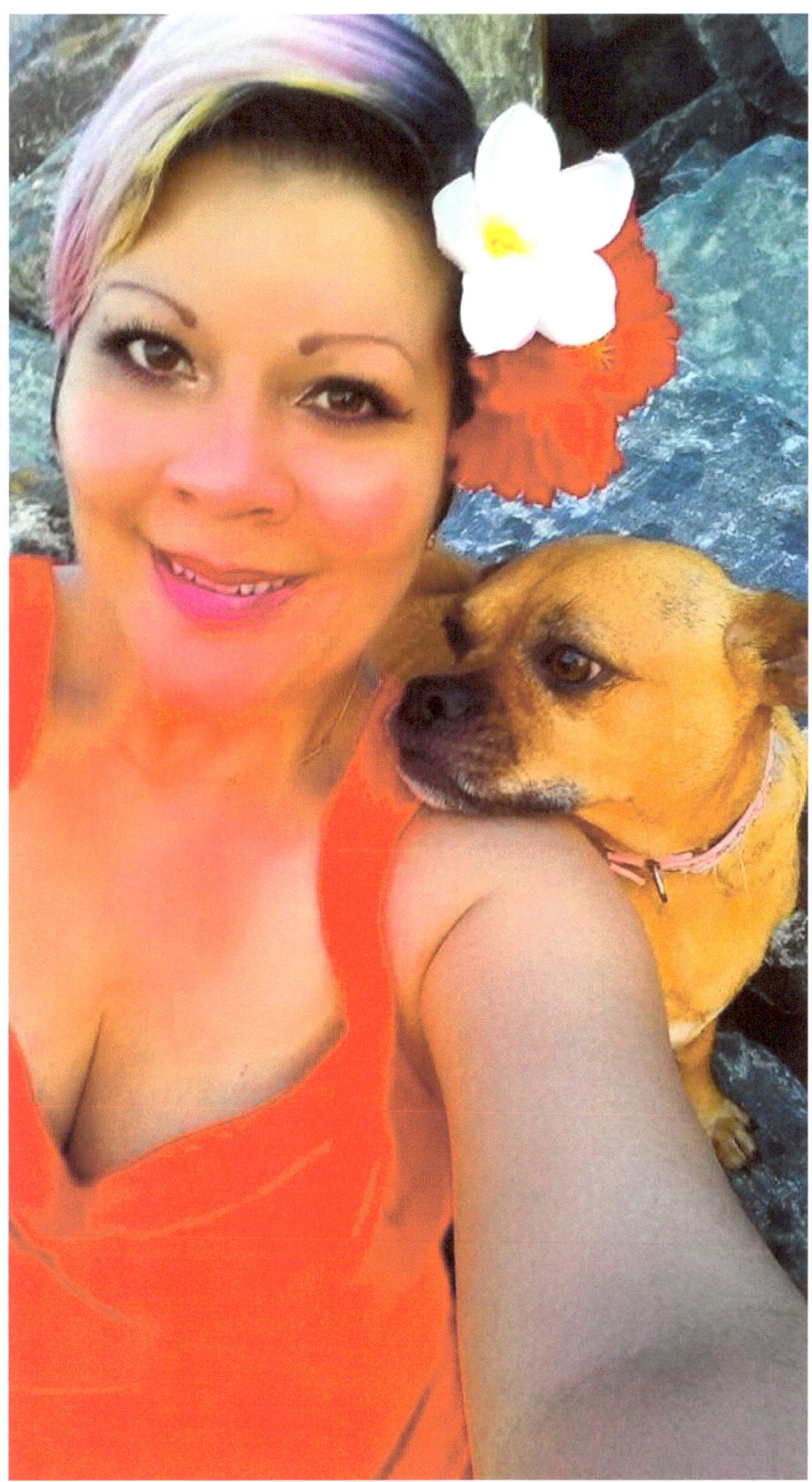

ABOUT THE AUTHOR

JENNENE CHRISTINE OBREMSKI IS A DIGITAL ARTIST, PHOTOGRAPHER, POET, AUTHOR, INTERPRETER AND DOCUMENT TRANSLATOR FOR HER NATIVE LANGUAGE CHUUKESE FROM MICRONESIA. SHE LIVES IN SOUTHERN MARYLAND WITH HER HUSBAND KEN AND 3 CHILDREN, ANDREA, ANTHONY AND JACOB AS WELL AS 3 DOGS (TYRONE, DANIELLE AND HER BEST FRIEND JOLIE), 2 CATS(VINCENT AND PAUL), A BUNNY (DONUT) AND A BEARDED DRAGON (LARRY). SHE ENJOYS DRIVING TO THE BEACH TO WATCH AND TAKE PICTURES OF THE SUNRISE WITH HER BUDDY JOLIE AT HER SIDE. JENNENE IS A SURVIVOR OF CHILD SEXUAL AND PHYSICAL ABUSE. SHE FINDS HEALING THROUGH HER DIGITAL ART AND HER WRITING. SHE HAS MORE BOOKS PUBLISHED ON CREATESPACE.COM AND AMAZON.COM.

www.ingramcontent.com/pod-product-compliance
Lightning Source LLC
Chambersburg PA
CBHW051826210526
45473CB00005B/1753